beside the sea

maritime style

Peter Ashley

ENGLISH HERITAGE

AN ENGLISH HERITAGE POCKET BOOK

p 1 **Lyme Regis** DORSET
Mooring buoys beached in the shelter of The Cobb.

p 2 **Eastbourne** EAST SUSSEX
A three flavour dummy ice cream, an appetising three-dimensional sign for an Ice Cream Parlour.

The James Bond quotation on page 63 is from *Goldfinger* by Ian Fleming
©Glidrose Productions Ltd., 1959

Published by English Heritage, Kemble Drive, Swindon SN2 2GZ
www.english-heritage.org.uk
English Heritage is the Government's statutory adviser on all aspects of the historic environment.

© Peter Ashley
Images © Peter Ashley

First published 2004

ISBN 1 85074 909 4

Product code 50963

British Library Cataloguing in Publication data
A CIP catalogue record for this book is available from the British Library.

Edited by Val Horsler
Page layout by Peter Ashley and Chuck Goodwin
Cover by Peter Ashley

Printed by Bath CPI

contents

introduction 6

sea views 8

pleasure domes 22

vantage points 36

today's catch 40

life savers 50

saintly shores 60

work details 64

lucky dips 74

introduction

What there is of English seaside building of the genuine sort should be watched with a jealous eye – even if it is only a matter of a few useful tarred sheds under a sheltering cliff.
The Nautical Style, John Piper

The development by man of the strip of land immediately behind the beach has, like the part designed by nature, assumed an almost incalculable variety of forms.
The English at the Seaside, Christopher Marsden

We are continually told we are a maritime nation. Salt water is supposed to run in our veins, and we are expected to go misty-eyed at pictures of tea clippers and galleons, even if we live in Tamworth. It must be to do with our close proximity to the coast, wherever we are. After all, even land-locked Tamworth is less than a hundred miles away from either a west or an east coast, as the seagull flies. Most of us are much nearer.

Our coastline has always been a place of work, with havens for fishing fleets, ports for sea-born trade and as the first line of defence against invasion. Today, much of it is sadly only a reminder of former glories, but the coast still has to defend us from ourselves, and there is thankfully always the welcome presence of lifeboat stations, lifeguard huts and coastguard lookouts. This isn't a tour of the coastline, more an inquisitive ramble along certain stretches of it to look at how we've responded to it in terms of buildings and nautical artefacts. Equally it isn't a listing of our maritime heritage, although our history as an island dictates much of what we will see.

Unless we have always lived by the sea, holidays and excursions will be our first experience of these things. My first sighting was from a taxi, moving across a flat green landscape from a lonely railway station towards a tiny row of 1930s bungalows, lined up to face the beach and the North Sea in Lincolnshire. Everybody's first time will be different, but it was the railways that opened up the idea of holidays for everyone. Until their tracks reached the coast, the seaside for pleasure had been the preserve of the rich taking cold baths for their health, hugely popularised by George III at Weymouth and by his son in Brighton. This royal patronage left an architectural legacy in both these towns, but soon all around the coast trains were steaming into stations with gulls screaming overhead. These trainsheds were quickly followed by grand hotels, arcaded shops and rows of terraced guest houses with names like Spinaker, Tamarisk and Harbour Lights. And then the pier: a chance to walk on the ocean and take in a show where the crash of breaking waves counterpointed a songstress belting out *When Father Papered the Parlour.*

The motor car aided and abetted the railway in the rise and rise of the seaside resort. A new breed of developer rubbed his hands as he wondered how many bungalows could be squeezed between one resort and the next. Holiday camps, retirement homes, amusement arcades and caravans (why can't they be painted in camouflage patterns?) eroded the landscape as surely as a tidal surge. The wake-up call came when we saw how much we were losing, and now many miles of coastline are protected, with English Heritage caring for buildings as varied as the shorelines themselves. They so deserve our proper care and attention, particularly, it has to be said, when it comes to looking after seaside piers.

sea views

Thorpeness SUFFOLK
In 1910 the hamlet of Thorpe, just north of Aldeburgh, was transformed into Thorpeness – an estate of half-timbered and weatherboarded houses where wealthy families could come to holiday, the children swept up in a kind of *Swallows and Amazons* existence on boating lakes. Most of it looks inwards to the jolliness of an imported windmill and the surreal House in the Clouds (see the following page), but the vernacular style is seen to great effect along the beach.

∧ **Birling Gap** EAST SUSSEX

Here the vertical chalk cliff summits of the Seven Sisters start their undulations westwards (although in fact there are eight of them), and the mass of Beachy Head rises up to the east. The Gap is threatened by coastal erosion, so this row of Victorian coastguard cottages is in constant peril of collapsing onto the beach. It was happening when Richard Jefferies came here in the early 1880s, and he made a very wise observation that all of us who live in perilous proximity to the waves should note: '...there is an infinite possibility about the sea; it may do what it is not recorded to have done'.

⌐ **Thorpeness** SUFFOLK

The 1920s House in the Clouds is not quite what it seems. The red 'house' is just a dummy covering for a water tower; the accommodation is in the weatherboarded base. Water was once pumped up into it by the little post mill opposite.

Holy Island NORTHUMBERLAND

Probably an unwelcome sea view if you're taking it in from this little tower. Holy Island has Lindisfarne at its southern tip, with its Priory and Lutyens-restored Castle, but it can only be reached with safety for 11 hours out of 24. The sandy sea bed is traversed by a scary causeway, usually still wet from a receding tide, and should you seriously mistime your run you'd better hope you are within reach of this weatherboarded refuge. Tide tables are an essential reference tool for residents and visitors, and the sea does come in frighteningly fast.

Scarborough NORTH YORKSHIRE

The Grand Hotel has seen grander days, but this 1867 old lady still dominates the seafront
at Scarborough, a truly Victorian statement of ultra-confidence by architect Cuthbert Brodick.
As with all buildings of such magnitude, the Grand has developed its own architectural mythology:
the four domes represent the seasons, there are 365 bedrooms and the whole yellow and red
brick edifice is in the shape of a 'V' for Victoria. It might all be true, but the 'V' is probably more to
do with its vertiginous site on a narrow section of clifftop.

These days the Grand caters more for pensioners disgorging from motor coaches than for mill owners heaving themselves out of Rolls Royces, but nothing diminishes the grandeur of its 13 storeys rising up from the beach and a magnificent staircase that tempts one to descend it in Fred Astaire hat 'n' cane style.

Worthing WEST SUSSEX

The railways not only brought the possibility of a seaside holiday within reach of millions, but were also responsible for developing the resorts themselves, even building some of them from scratch. In 1900–9 the London, Brighton & South Coast Railway issued nearly 19 million excursion tickets. Some of those tickets would have been in the pockets of coats hung up behind the doors in this still classic row of guest houses on the Worthing seafront – a cosy but slightly unnerving world of pink candlewick toilet seat covers and bottles of Daddies Sauce.

Wells-next-the-Sea NORFOLK

Beach huts have evolved in much the same way as we're supposed to have done, starting out in the sea and ending up at the top of the beach. These gaily painted wooden huts are the successors of the bathing machines our Victorian ancestors tiptoed gingerly out of at the water's edge. Modesty finally being overcome, the bathing machine was parked up for good, losing its wheels and gaining a permanent place on the beach. Apparently you're not allowed to sleep in a beach hut overnight, they cost a fortune and there's a waiting list a coastline long.

Southwold SUFFOLK

Part of the beach huts' charm is that they are invariably in rows stretched out along promenades or at the furthest reach of the tide. Individuality then creeps in with the paint schemes (I love the bathing suit stripes of 'Victoria' below) and the names. A friend of mine lounges about on a hot mountainside in Italy dreaming of owning one back in Blighty just so that he can call it Spindrift. This Southwold row also made an appearance with Judi Dench in the biopic *Iris*.

Whitstable KENT

Whitstable was once the port for Canterbury, and
certainly its proximity to the mouth of the Swale and
therefore access to the Medway gave it strategic
importance. Out on the horizon can be seen the
menacing shapes of the Maunsell forts on their tall iron
legs, but back on shore it's oysters and higgledy-piggledy
buildings scattered along the beach like painted driftwood.
This is the fishing quarter, with tarred sheds, weatherboarded cottages and upturned boats lying amongst the
hardy seashore plants.

Old Hunstanton NORFOLK

These rows of chalets are a perfect illustration of coastal accretion. We hear much about the opposite, with tides dramatically eating away at the coastline, but all the eroded material doesn't disappear into salty thin air. What the sea takes away, the sea deposits somewhere else, and complicated tide movements have built up sand dune banks here on the north Norfolk coast.

The first row of beach huts is where the pines darken the horizon. As deposits of sand grew, so tough marram grass got a grip and the coastline shifted another few yards. Successive beach hut owners have colonised the next vantage point like tourists fighting over sun beds.

pleasure domes

Scarborough NORTH YORKSHIRE
*Let Epsom, Tunbridge, Barnet, Knaresborough be
In what request they will, Scarborough for me.*

Such was the fame of new spa waters discovered
here in 1626, that Scarborough was visited 71 years
later by the intrepid traveller Celia Fiennes who
found the supposedly efficacious spring water
bubbling up in a well on the beach – a well that was
often washed by the tides, prompting her to note
that the sea water left '…*a brackish and saltness
which makes it purge pretty much*…'. I bet.

Below the South Cliff is a more permanent reminder
of the status Scarborough held with those who
sought all its plunging and gurgling benefits. Verity and
Hunt's 1880 Spa Building with its French pavilion
roof sits within a purging jet's arc of the original well,
right on the beach with its own promenade and
extended in 1925 with a gracious conservatory-like
ballroom.

Now it's called the Spa Complex, which means it can
be everything from a conference centre to a venue
for tribute bands, but alas no longer a restorative
refuge where strange things can be done to you
with rubber hosepipes in echoing tiled bathrooms.

Great Yarmouth NORFOLK

The Wellington Pier is where I first saw
Benny Hill. Not in person, but as a giant
babyface cut out of plywood and stuck
onto the entrance. The original pier was
designed in 1853 by an Eastern Counties
Railway engineer, Peter Ashcroft, with the
pavilions added by J W Cockrill 50 years
later. Much of his decorative panelling and
niceties has gone, leaving a kind of sad
boarded-up feel that probably even
Singalongamax can't help. But it's fared
better than the Britannia Pier to the
north. Built four years later, the Britannia
was promptly cut in half by a schooner
and then burnt down three times.

Clevedon NORTH SOMERSET

Clevedon is gothic and Italianate villas set amidst flowering shrubs and ilex trees, ornamented lamp posts and a Victorian pier on spindly wrought iron legs paddling in the Severn estuary. It was built in 1868, recycling rails salvaged from one of Brunel's railways, but was closed in 1970 after suffering the ignominy of losing a 200-foot section during a load-bearing test. It was nearly dismantled, but local protest, grants and fundraising brought this unique and delicate pier back to fully restored life. As the restoration started, stocks of Brunel's rails were discovered in some long-forgotten store.

∧ > **Eastbourne** EAST SUSSEX

One name keeps cropping up when it comes to piers: Eugenious Birch.
A bit of an engineering child prodigy, he was able to put his skills to
good use in the rapidly developing railway age. After doing much the
same in India, he returned to concentrate on bridges and viaducts, just
as the possibilities of their design principles were being recognised for
marine construction. Birch saw a bright new future for the seaside pier,
and, starting with Margate in 1851, he was responsible for 14 piers
over the next 30 years. Eastbourne opened in 1872, 1,000 feet long
with cast-iron screw piles supporting the 60ft-wide iron and wood
frame.

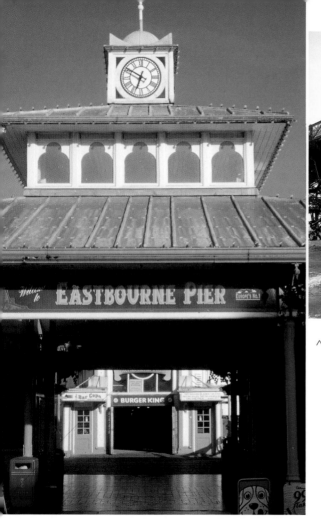

∧ **Brighton** EAST SUSSEX

Despite all the well-meaning action groups and promises from local authorities, this is what happened to the West Pier. Would it perhaps be kinder to let the old lady go and then build something of equal appeal for our own age? Watch Richard Attenborough's film of *Oh! What a Lovely War* to see just how stunning she was in the late 1960s.

Great Yarmouth NORFOLK

A little Crystal Palace by the sea, brought here from
Torquay in 1903 to become the Winter Gardens. The
stepped and pyramid-roofed glass structure was first
erected on the Devon coast in 1878–81 for £13,000.
Yarmouth Corporation paid £1,300 for it. Imagine
being an Edwardian here, walking amongst humid ferns
and water lilies with the East Anglian light greenly
filtering down through the leaves, just yards away the
cold German Ocean thumping up onto the beach.

Lowestoft SUFFOLK

There is a book to be done about buildings that have faces. I've started a collection that includes a lighthouse in Northumberland and a linen mill in Ireland. I so want this sailing club to be in it, but does the third middle window disqualify it? This is the Royal Norfolk & Suffolk Yacht Club on the quayside in Lowestoft where if you listen very carefully you can hear the constant chink-chink of ice cubes dropping into big gin and tonics.

Burnham-on-Crouch ESSEX

Another royal yacht club, but this time with a beautiful iron staircase for the commodore to ascend to his observation deck. And carefully cut-out iron letters for the club's initials.

∧ **Bexhill** EAST SUSSEX
Urbane ocean liner sophistication like this must have caused a few nervous
flutters in the Bexhill of the 1930s, like seeing a bright young thing do the
Palais Glide across a bowling green. The resort was developed in the 1880s by
Lord De La Warr, and this is the De La Warr Pavilion, a concrete, steel and
glass cocktail by Erich Mendelsohn and Serge Chermayeff. De La Warr is
pronounced as Delaware, the American state.

< Opposite is this equally surprising domed and columned pavilion, something
one would expect to find in Arcadia surrounded by cypress trees and
centaurs. It fits perfectly into the seaside tradition that allows bold statements
to be made just for fun.

One of the most ubiquitous seaside buildings is the shelter, a place for getting out of the wind, out of the sun, reading the morning paper or just staring out to sea. Here is a sample that have more visual appeal than the usual glorified bus shelters.

⌐ **Mundesley** NORFOLK
The Edwardian Golf Club Style. Terracotta ridge tiles and brick in-filling.

∧ **Hastings** EAST SUSSEX
The Gothic Railway Style. Warm orange Sussex roof-tiling and church porch windows.

< **Cromer** NORFOLK
The Cricket Pavilion Style. Norfolk reed thatch and elegant stucco columns.

⌐ **Cromer** NORFOLK
The Regency Style. Classical round-headed windows and railings to stop sudden uncontrolled lurches to the cliff edge.

Clevedon NORTH SOMERSET

Sea shanties and music hall favourites come and go on the breeze as the band strikes up in this beautifully restored 1887 bandstand amongst the wind-bent evergreens on Clevedon's gently undulating promenade.

Weymouth DORSET

Another day of murder, wife battering and police harassment is about to start on the beach at Weymouth. Round the back of his candy-striped portable theatre the Punch & Judy man (or 'professor' as his craft calls him) prepares for a show that has its roots in Roman times, but more recognisably in the *commedia dell'arte* travelling shows in 17th-century Italy. Pulcinella became Punch when this sinister character arrived on the streets of London during the Restoration, probably a welcome relief after the rigours of humourless Puritanism.

Whitstable KENT

I don't think you can buy a pint of bitter nearer to the sea than this, pier bars excepted. The weatherboarded Old Neptune is as at home here on the beach as the yachts and boats pulled up on to the shingle, a wonderfully evocative pub where on a stormy winter's night you'd expect characters from a Charles Dickens novel to burst in and lay a drowned sailor out on the wooden floorboards.

vantage points

Lyme Regis DORSET

Little towers and cupolas were essential elements in
the maritime style. Merchants looked out for
returning cargoes and fishermen for signs of their
livelihood as shoals shaded the sea and . . . well, who
really needs an excuse just to sit and gaze at it all?

The Philpot Museum in Bridge Street, Lyme Regis,
was designed in 1901 by G B Vialls. Here on the
seafront is a delightful mixture of styles with 17th-
century Dutch meeting the Victorian. It's topped out
with a polygonal brick rotunda that supports a
cupola that would look equally at home on a
provincial town hall. A perfect place for a Thomas
Hardy heroine to look out for the return of a sea
captain.

Upnor KENT

English Heritage looks after an Elizabethan gun fort here, a 16th-century castle built to protect Queen Elizabeth I's warships riding at anchor in the reaches of the Medway. Opposite the gateway is this little look-out tower that looks much older than it actually is. In reality it's a conservatory on a tile-hung base built around 1900. As a gentleman told me at the castle 'What a lovely place to sit with your breakfast egg and toast soldiers watching the shipping.'

Scarborough NORTH YORKSHIRE

Scarborough gathers around two bays, North and Sou divided by the castle on its promontory. Until 1908 the was no direct seaward link between them. The Marine Drive took 11 years to construct, carving its way roun underneath the castle and entered from the south thr this Toll House. Pevsner got sniffy about it in his *Buildin of England*, calling it phoney, but I think it's one of the b things on the seafront, a Norman Shaw-style gatehous with a ground floor of stone and an upper storey of b infilled timber-framing. And an eyecatcher of a tower, o put to use by the coastguard.

Newquay CORNWALL

Up here above the harbour is a remnant of Newquay's less garish past, when in the 18th and 19th centuries the sea was netted for vast quantities of pilchards. This is the Huer's House, where the ocean was watched for the red stain in the water that indicated a shoal. The cry 'Huer! Huer!' (presumably carrying further than 'pilchard! pilchard!') from the lookout alerted the fishermen below to launch their boats.

today's catch

< **Port Isaac** CORNWALL

Fishing is still a serious business in Port Isaac, a Cornish village that is mercifully neither over-commercialised nor over-run with Lycra-clad surfers. Which is probably why it was chosen as the location for television's *Doc Martin*, standing in for the fictitious Port Wen. Here you can walk about amongst the boats as they tilt on the beach, and then treat yourself to large crabs and lobsters in a wet-floored shop ventilated by a salty wind blowing straight through from the pounding waves that surge against the harbour wall.

↘ **Birling Gap** EAST SUSSEX

In the absence of convenient natural harbours fishermen take their chances with launching boats directly into the sea from the beach. There are only two openings through the mighty chalk cliffs that stretch from Seaford to Eastbourne, at Cuckmere Haven and, even narrower, here at Birling Gap. It was once perfect for smugglers bringing in contraband, shadowy figures hurrying along the lane across the downs, melting away in the village of East Dean. Kipling's *Five and twenty ponies / Trotting through the dark- / Brandy for the Parson, / 'Baccy for the Clerk...*

Hastings EAST SUSSEX

The rise and fall of the tides at Hastings is so high that the fishermen have to haul their boats right to the top of the beach, called here The Stade, to ensure they're above the high water mark. Under the cliffs are their net-drying sheds; tall, tarred or creosoted weatherboarded towers huddling protectively round the Fishermen's Church. Tall to contain their equipment, narrow to minimise the rent paid on the ground. Sometimes called 'deezes' or 'tackle boxes', one or two are over 300 years old.

Whitstable KENT

Oysters are a religion in Whitstable, and here on the beach is one of their cathedrals, the Royal Native Oyster Stores. The building is a treat both inside and out. Shingle-coloured brick perfectly sets off the green shutters and the white weatherboarded bay window, whilst inside the levering-open of oyster shells and the snap of crabs' legs echo in rooms breezily at home in a perfect seaside setting.

Dunwich SUFFOLK

'Like the tales of the Lost Atlantis and the mythical land of Lyonnesse, the story of Dunwich seizes upon the imagination; though when one sees how little remains of what may once have been the chief city of East Anglia it is difficult to believe that Dunwich, too, was not a phantom city of a land of dreams.' Highways & Byways in East Anglia, William Dutt

A row of fishermens' huts, a handful of houses and a pub down the lane from the beach, and that's it. But in medieval England this was a prosperous seaport with at least eight parish churches and a population praying, fishing, shipbuilding and desperately trying to keep the sea at bay. Now there is no trace of the Dunwich that is under the sea. Of course, they say that on stormy nights you can hear the bells tolling under the waves, and on such a night that's not difficult to imagine. Within living memory there was still the gaunt outline of the last church, All Saints, up on the crumbling low cliffs. In 1970 I saw the last piece of masonry being claimed by the tide.

Holy Island NORTHUMBERLAND

Maritime recycling on the beach at Lindisfarne. A very appropriate way to keep alive the memory of the fishing boats that gave sterling service to the fishermen of this north-east coast. Turn them upside down, put a door in the stern and you've got an equipment store.

Aldeburgh SUFFOLK

The soundtrack for Aldeburgh is the first of Benjamin Britten's Sea Interludes from
Peter Grimes. If you play it at home you are immediately transported back amongst
the ice-cream-coloured houses, tarred fishermens' huts and rusty winches on the
shingle. All on the edge of a restless sea and about as East Anglian seaside
vernacular as it's possible to get. The town slowly metamorphosed from its Tudor
heyday as a shipbuilding town at the mouth of the Alde to a quiet Suffolk resort
with just a handful of fishermen working from the beach. Evidence of its former
prestige and indeed size can be seen in the herringboned brick Moot Hall on the
seafront that once stood in the original market place at the centre of the town. The
indigenous patterns of Aldeburgh's fabric are now added to by the blue and white
striped shirt material favoured by the cognescenti at the eponymous music festival.

∧ Maggie Hambling's scallop shell memorial to Britten looks like a hybrid sea creature progressing in a crab-like crawl down to the waves. Cue for plaintive discordant squeals from an oboe. There's been a bit of a rumpus over it being here at all, and of course being modern art someone had to throw a can of paint over it. I think it's perfect, not just for its beautifully steely shells and cut-out quotation from Peter Grimes, but for it's location on a deserted stretch of beach away from the town and its art police.

DANGER
NO BATHING

PERYGL
DIM YMDROCHI

BARMOUTH
FERRY
START
11 - AM

life savers

Fairbourne GWYNEDD

The sea is a cruel place for the unwary. Holidaymakers not used to the vagaries of strong currents and changeable weather can quickly get into serious trouble, even if they're swimming just offshore or stretched out on a Lilo. If they're lucky a trained lifeguard will impress everybody with a dramatic save, but it could equally mean the local lifeboat crew turning out. For the mariner it's a different kettle of fish, as it were. Even the most experienced sailors can get caught out by rapidly deteriorating conditions and in addition to satellite positioning still benefit from navigational lights and the watchful eye of the coastguard. Let's hope they don't get replaced by a call centre computer in Dunstable.

More benignly, safety at sea means we can enjoy the colourful spare geometry of the nautical style from dry land, as here in Barmouth Bay at Fairbourne.

South Gare REDCAR & CLEVELAND

Corrugated iron painted in red oxide is something of a ubiquitous seaside building material, used where the practicalities of function and corrosive salt water take precedence over aesthetic considerations. There is, however, something very uncompromising about these rippling iron sheets that has a certain appeal. This is the no-nonsense way of prefabricating a building, with curved sections instantly giving an arched roof like a Dutch barn or a military Romney hut.

Wells-next-the-Sea NORFOLK

The first lifeboat station I saw here was a wood and corrugated iron affair, the cream and maroon paint so faded by the sunlight that it was starting to become part of the shingly beach. Its replacement works equally as well, the architect respecting what was here before by keeping the corrugated effect and choosing colours from the paint card that, whilst echoing its predecessor in looking good on the beach, recognises its function as an emergency service.

∧ **Rye Harbour** EAST SUSSEX

The salty business end of Rye is Rye Harbour, an unkempt jumble of cottages and sheds dotted about on the mud at the side of the River Rother where it tips out into Rye Bay. The lifeboat station is comparatively new, but again – what a good idea – the blue walls and white window frames have been painted to echo a signal flag.

> **Portland** DORSET

This white Egyptian-style obelisk was erected by Trinity House in 1844 as a sea mark to warn of a dangerous shelf of rock immediately below the cliff edge. It stands a little way from the magnificent red and white striped lighthouse at Portland Bill.

∧ **Kings Lynn** NORFOLK

Facing the setting sun and the estuary of the River
Ouse are painted buoys waiting to be taken out
onto the treacherous channels of the Wash. Their
sheer size, bright colours and shapes make them
one of the very best examples of the nautical style.

The Wash sees the outfall of a number of rivers
that run down from the watershed of central
England: the Witham, the Welland, the Nene and
the Great Ouse, all emptying into this curious, almost
square area of sea. The channels and sandbanks hide
any number of mysteries in their names: Thief Sand,
Clay Hole, Roaring Middle, Scotsman's Sled. And a
light beacon called Big Annie.

> **Dungeness** KENT

There have been five lighthouses at Dungeness and indeed this whole area of shifting shingle has a very temporary air about it with oddly-placed shacks, beached fishing boats and leaning electricity poles. And in and out of it all the little tracks of the Romney, Hythe & Dymchurch Light Railway. This is the 1904 lighthouse, 143 feet high and made redundant when the insensitively-designed nuclear power station blocked its light. At its side is the base of Wyatt's 1792 lighthouse, subsequently used for keepers' housing.

∨ **Happisburgh** NORFOLK

Like a primitive painting the red and white simplicity of the 1791 Happisburgh lighthouse sits out in the lonely fields next to a particularly barren curve of the Norfolk coastline. It is very noteworthy in being the only privately-operated lighthouse in the United Kingdom after Trinity House abandoned it in 1987.

∨ **Brixham** DEVON

The Berry Head lighthouse perches on a precipitous mass of jackdaw-haunted sandstone.

It is a perfect example of Trinity House's style of immaculately maintained buildings painted in the house colours of brilliant white and green with a full colour embossed crest. I asked them what shade of green they call it and they said 'Trinity House Green'.

< **Tollesbury** ESSEX

Walking over the footpaths that cross the little creeks that sidle off the River Blackwater brings you to this red ex-lightship *Trinity*, rising and falling with the tide in Woodrolfe Creek. We are more likely these days to see lightships moored up in harbours as floating bars and restaurants than standing guard over shipping hazards, and indeed *Trinity* is admirably adapted by Fellowship Afloat into an outdoor activity centre.

∨ **Southwold** SUFFOLK

A very English style of lifeguard post, a converted beach hut up on the promenade. Here in Southwold the hut for pinning up resuscitation diagrams is painted bright yellow with an emergency-style red stripe and practical stencilled letters.

saintly shores

Bradwell-on-Sea ESSEX

Thankfully you still have to walk the last half mile to discover one of Britain's oldest and loneliest churches, facing the mouth of the Blackwater on the tip of the Dengie Peninsular. This gives you time for a bit of contemplation amongst the cornfields and wild flowers before the door is finally opened into the cool, dark interior. Time to remember that these stones and bricks were brought here from the nearby ruinous Roman fort of *Othona* almost 1,400 years ago. The chapel was founded by St Cedd, a missionary from the north, but its dedication is 'St Peter's-on-the-Wall'. Before its reconsecration in 1920 the building had served as a navigational sea-mark and as a local farmer's barn, which explains its remarkable survival.

Reculver KENT

The landmark towers of Reculver appear between Herne Bay and Margate on the site of a monastery built where the Roman fort of *Regulbium* guarded the northern end of the Wantsum Channel that divided the Isle of Thanet from the mainland. (The southern end was at Richborough.) The rest of the church of St Mary was demolished in 1809, but these towers survived because of their usefulness to Trinity House as a navigational aid. Recycled Roman building materials, particularly the red tile-like bricks, can still be seen in the walls.

James Bond knows Reculver. He brought his battleship grey Aston Martin DB3 down the A2 to visit Auric Goldfinger at Thanet Alloys, '…*holding the racing wheel on a light rein, listening to the relaxed purr of the exhausts.*' …until '*He came up with a crossroads. To the left the signpost said RECULVER. Underneath was the ancient monument sign for Reculver church. Bond slowed, but didn't stop. No hanging about. He motored slowly on, keeping his eyes open.*'

work details

Kings Lynn NORFOLK

This Customs House is a film star. It appeared with Al Pacino in *Revolution*, pretending to be in Boston, Massachusetts. It deserved to be; this is one of the best late 17th-century buildings in England. It was built by local merchant Henry Bell in 1683 as a Merchants' Exchange, but bought by the Collector of Customs in 1718. The ground floor was once an open space accessed through the now filled-in arches.(Abingdon Town Hall gives a good idea of how it would have looked.) King Charles II stares down in approval from his niche underneath the crisply-painted wooden cupola.

It stands on Purfleet Quay, and not long ago had a gigantic grain silo overshadowing it, with the quay so silted up with mud it appeared to be devouring the remains of a wooden boat. The silo has gone, and the scrubbed-up quay can once again, on special occasions, receive boats from the Ouse.

Chatham KENT

The associations of these dockyards are a roll call of over four centuries of naval history. Henry VII established them with a store for servicing his fleet in the Medway; Drake, Hawkins and Nelson sailed out from here and the latter's flagship *HMS Victory* was built here. The Royal Navy abandoned ship in 1984, but it thankfully has a new life as a fascinating museum.

The long boat-shaped shed is a covered slipway built in 1835, and the cream-painted wooden buildings that now house the shop and a cafe are perfect examples of the shipshape naval style.

∧ **Great Yarmouth** NORFOLK

I've always thought of ships as architecture that goes to sea. After all they're still buildings for housing crew, cargoes and navigational equipment, albeit built of steel and with a propensity to sway about a bit. The *Putford Rover* is moored up here on the more subdued side of Great Yarmouth that is South Quay, a frequent visitor that ferries equipment and supplies out to the North Sea oil rigs.

> **River Thames** LONDON

HMS Belfast has long been one of London's prime tourist attractions, as popular and indeed almost as permanent as St Pauls and nearby Tower Bridge. I know next to nothing about naval vessels, but this is deeply impressive. Great slabs of 'don't mess with me' steel and armaments in functional matt paint, the stark outlines broken up by the giant abstract shapes of deep grey camouflage.

∧ **Dartford** KENT

A big cargo ship waits up on the Thames Estuary in front of the Queen Elizabeth Bridge at Dartford. A sea-going logo if ever there was one.

∧ **Tollesbury** ESSEX

I love this forgotten corner of Essex, where there is no clearly defined edge between land and sea.
A map reveals it to be a coastline of saltings and muddy channels, merging and blurring all the way from
Harwich to Canvey Island. Where the road finally starts to give out at Tollesbury these buildings appear,
perfectly at home here with their marine-style outside ladders. They were built in 1902 as sail lofts, big
enough for drying off and storing the sails of 'J' class or 'Jumbo' racing yachts. They fulfil other purposes
now, but everywhere here the inheritors of this watery landscape can be found working on their boats.

> **Faversham** KENT

This storehouse on Faversham Creek is known locally as the 'Big Building'. It was built between 1843 and
1845 as a hop store when the creek was improved. The effect of its bulk is all the more pronounced by
its comparative isolation. The painted lettering gives a couple of clues about the considerable trade that
Faversham handled, to which could be added grain and bricks, flour and fruit, vegetables and gunpowder.

> **Newlyn** CORNWALL

Newlyn is very much a working harbour. This is not the picturesque ideal of weatherbeaten Cornish fishermen in knitted jumpers, mending their nets and pointing out to sea with the stems of clay pipes. No, Newlyn is throbbing marine engines in hard-bitten trawlers and that unmistakeable stench of gutted fish and diesel oil. But art has found its way here just as emphatically as it did with the Edwardian painters of the Newlyn School (Frank Bramley's *A Hopeless Dawn*). A smart fishing boat makes steady progress through a choppy sea on the side of an oil tank.

>> **Kings Lynn** NORFOLK

Harbourside buildings are now discovering new uses; here's one waiting to be brought back to life, but in the meantime adding a vibrant addition to the jolly paint schemes on the South Quay. Kings Lynn is no longer the busy East Anglian port that brought the town prosperity, but boats do come in from the North Sea, and underneath a giant dockside elevator can still be found grain spillages. But the once thriving quayside is emasculated into serving as a promenade, with marked-out car park spaces now instead of cargoes of orange Dutch roof pantiles and Delft tea services in straw-packed cases.

lucky dips

< **Great Yarmouth** NORFOLK
Nelson's Column without Nelson. At 144 feet
high it is a foot less than the column in
Trafalgar Square, but was erected only 12
years after Nelson's death, as opposed to the
35 years it took for his monument to tower
over Trafalgar Square. William Wilkins' design
has the Victories in caryatid fashion supporting
a statue of Britannia, who, in recognition of the
town's importance as a seaport, faces west
across the harbour. Looking at it today,
surrounded as the column is by dereliction
that includes a defunct gasworks, it is hard to
imagine that Britannia once looked down on
the pleasures of a seaside racecourse.

<< **Holkham** NORFOLK
Equipment ready to build the seaside
architecture that is at once the most popular
and the most temporary.

Aldeburgh SUFFOLK

We can't leave the coast without looking at a Martello Tower. The fear of a Napoleonic invasion in the late 18th century prompted the first large-scale building of coastal defences since the reign of Henry VIII. The south east was naturally the most vulnerable and as a result, between 1804 and 1812, 103 Martello Towers were built, from here in Aldeburgh to Seaford in Sussex. They look like giant childrens' sandcastles, tipped out at the sea's edge with walls 13 feet thick. The roof held a twenty-four pounder cannon on a rotating platform. The inspiration and name came from the impregnable Torre della Mortella fort north of Corsica.

∧ **Hastings** EAST SUSSEX

The East Hill Lift rises up from the old town through the sandstone cliff, the second steepest cliff railway in Britain with a gradient of 2.8. Built in 1902, there's a very attractive tile-hung station at the bottom and an airy country park at the top.

> **Grange-over-Sands** CUMBRIA

Which railway station is nearest the sea? Dawlish in Devon must be a contender, and some, like Ryde on the Isle of Wight, are on piers, but Grange-over-Sands, looking out over Morecambe Bay, wins for a bracing seaside atmosphere.

acknowledgements

Val Horsler and Rob Richardson at English Heritage, Dr Arthur Percival in Faversham,
The Historic Dockyard at Chatham, Thames Europort in Dartford, Lucy Bland, Margaret Shepherd,
Chuck Goodwin, Rupert Farnsworth and Biff Raven-Hill.
The James Bond quotation on page 63 is from Goldfinger by Ian Fleming ©Glidrose Productions Ltd., 1959

bibliography

The Buildings of England Series, Penguin, Yale University Press
The Shell County Guides, Faber & Faber
The Nautical Style, Eric de Mare, Architectural Press, 1973
David Gentleman's Coastline, Weidenfeld & Nicolson, 1988
English Harbours & Coastal Villages, Christopher Somerville and John Bethell, Weidenfeld & Nicolson, 1989
Pavilions on the Sea, Cyril Bainbridge, Robert Hale, 1986
The Batsford Companion to Local History, Stephen Friar, Batsford, 1991

The John Piper quotation in the introduction is from 'The Nautical Style', in *Buildings and Prospects,*
The Architectural Press, 1948
The English at the Seaside by Christopher Marsden was published by Collins in 1947

< A detail from a lithographed cover for a Social and Holiday Guide issued in 1948 for the London County Council Staff Association. Evocative seaside imagery from the same style book as classic pre-war railway posters.

Overleaf:
Maldon ESSEX Speed limit buoys stacked on the quay like market stall grapefruit.